GEORGE MACDONALD

The Seeking Heart

GEORGE MACDONALD

The Seeking Heart

Kathy Triggs

Pickering Paperbacks

First published 1984
by Pickering & Inglis,
3 Beggarwood Lane,
Basingstoke, Hants RG23 7LP
United Kingdom.

ISBN 0 7208 0559 7

Text set by PRG TypoGraphics, Cheddar, Somerset.
Printed in Great Britain by
Richard Clay (The Chaucer Press) Ltd,
Bungay, Suffolk

Contents

1   The Seeking Heart
(1824-1853)

George MacDonald was born at a time when religious differences were strongly felt. His grandmother hated Roman Catholicism, though she was hopeful for those who had been 'misled'. She once read in the newspaper that there was a new Pope, and remarked, *'I have been prayin' to the Lord a' nicht to gie him a new hert an' a guid wife.'*

The family lived in Huntly, a small town in what is now the Grampian region of Scotland. They were of Celtic origin. Their ancestors had been Roman

Catholics, but by the time George MacDonald's grandfather married, they had become protestants. His wife Isabella was a zealous evangelical protestant, and she was to exert a great deal of influence on her sons and grandsons. Her husband died relatively young, leaving his bleaching business together with a thread-making factory to his three sons George, Charles and James. Charles also inherited a bank agency from his father, but it did him little good. He began to speculate with the savers' money, ran heavily into debt, and finally had to flee to America.

In 1822 George (the father of the preacher/novelist) married Helen MacKay and took her to live in a house which he had built for himself in the centre of Huntly. Helen was well educated, intelligent and beautiful; her best friend said in later years that she and her husband were the most beautiful man and woman she had ever seen. A miniature portrait done just after the marriage shows her to have dark, glossy hair, fine eyes and a delicate mouth. Her husband was said to be *'As fine a man as might be seen in four parishes,'* well-built and robust.

Their first two sons were born in the Huntly House, Charles in 1823 and George, our subject, on the tenth of December 1824. In 1822 his father and uncles had leased from the fourth Duke of Gordon land and farm buildings known as 'The Farm', about half a mile outside the town. They wanted The Farm for the sake of its fields which sloped down to the River Bogie. Linen could be spread out here for the sunlight to complete the bleaching process.

In 1826 George and James built a house at The Farm and moved their families into it. The house is still there today. It is rather small, considering that it was shared by two families. Four more boys were born to George and Helen: James, Alexander, John MacKay who died in infancy, and John Hill. In addition James had a daughter, Margaret, and a son, James. Box-beds were installed in some of the living-rooms to provide space. The family had a tendency to tuberculosis, and the close quarters at which they lived must have fostered its spread. Helen Mac-Donald died in 1832 of tuberculosis, when young George was eight years old. Although in later life he could remember little about her, he adored her memory. The bereavement may have been made easier for the boys by the long period when their mother was ill. During this time they had to keep away from the house to give her as much quiet as possible, and so saw very little of her. After her death they were looked after by their aunt, Christina Mac-Kay. Her love and devotion made a lasting impression on them.

There were two schools in Huntly, the parish church school and the Adventure School, to which the MacDonald boys went. Young George, however, suffered from frequent attacks of bronchitis and asthma, and was often kept at home. He had caught the family disease and was to suffer throughout his long life from inflammations and haemorrhages of the lungs.

The teacher at the Adventure School was the Rev Colin Stewart, a man with a vicious sense of justice, whose thrashing were supposed, at least by his brothers, to have caused the death of young James at the age of eight. No doubt tuberculosis also played its part. George MacDonald later portrayed Stewart as Murdoch Malison, the barbarous schoolmaster in *Alec Forbes of Howglen*. He gave him a timely repentance and heroic death – no doubt he hoped that Stewart himself would repent and be saved.

Despite his illnesses, his teacher, and the loss of his mother George MacDonald on the whole had a happy childhood. The boys roamed free in the summer holidays, partly because of the need to keep the house quiet for their mother. In any case their father was not a severe disciplinarian; in fact he was more inclined to smile than to scold if complaints were made about his boys' exploits. But he was really angry with them if they were guilty of any cruelty or injustice. He was not demonstrative, but had a deep love for them, and they in turn revered him. He was brave, patient and generous, with a fine sense of humour. His son portrayed him as the title character in his first successful novel, *David Elginbrod*. He emerges as a man of profound and original insight into the nature of God's love. He is described thus:

> *His carriage was full of dignity and a certain rustic refinement; his voice was wonderfully gentle, but deep; and slowest when most impassioned. He seemed to have come of some gigantic antediluvian breed: there was something of the Titan slumbering about him. He would have been a stern man, but for an unusual amount of reverence that seemed to overflood the sternness, and change it into strong love. No one had ever seen him thoroughly angry; his simple displeasure with any of the labourers, the quality of whose work was deficient, would go further than the laird's oaths.'*

Books were not easy to come by in such a remote Scottish town, but what there were young George read avidly, lying on the sofa in wintry days when his weak chest kept him away from school, or in the summer holidays lying on the broad back of his favourite horse, Missy, as she cropped the grass. The books he particularly mentions in connection with his childhood are such as even an adult would find heavy going today. There was *Pilgrim's Progress, Paradise Lost* and Klopstock's *Messiah* – an English translation of a German epic poem written in imitation of Milton. Also the Bible, in the Authorised Version, and probably the plays of Shakespeare. MacDonald's works reveal an intimate knowledge of both.

Isabella MacDonald's family had at first attended the parish (ie. Presbyterian) church. But the preaching there was not to her liking and eventually she betook herself and her family to the Congregational Church. This was newly established in the town. The denomination was also known at that time as 'the Independents', or as 'the Missionar Kirk' because of its evangelising zeal. Her son George became a deacon of this church, and every Monday morning he would visit the minister for prayer and fellowship. He himself was of a calm and cheerful temperament; he had learned to place his trust in the 'Good Shepherd of the sheep'. But his mother's faith was of a more sombre nature. She saw many things as sinful. She even thought that it was sinful to sing on the Sabbath except in church. Her grandson included a portrait of her in his novel *Robert Falconer*, as the old grandmother Mrs Falconer. She was greatly grieved by the backsliding of her son Charles — the one who had fled to America — and did actually burn his violin, as described in the novel, lest it lead anyone else astray. She believed that her son was beyond the reach of Divine Grace, and that it was sinful in her to continue to love and to pray for him.

Her beliefs were fostered by Scottish Calvinism, which emphasised the sovereignty of God's will to the point of saying that only those whom God has chosen − his 'elect' − can be saved. The rest are beyond the reach of God's grace and are doomed to hell for eternity. She felt that this was scriptural and therefore indisputable, however harsh and unfair it might seem. Man cannot hope to understand, much less oppose, the will of God.

Even as a boy her grandson could see the inconsistency in this belief. His grandmother's misery over her 'lost' son showed him that her love for him was greater than that she supposed God to have for him. The thoughtful, sensitive child began to understand that God's love must be very great, and must involve him in sufferings for his 'lost sheep' greater than those of his grandmother for his uncle.

In 1835 Mr Stewart left the Adventure School to emigrate to Australia. His place was taken by the Rev Alex Millar, a very different kind of man. He recognised the latent ability in young George, and gave encouragement and advice which resulted in his going for coaching to the Aulton Grammar School, Aberdeen. This was in 1840, when he was fifteen years old. It was a time of change for him, for in the previous year his father had married Margaret McColl, who had been the best friend of Helen Mac-

Donald. She too was from a family of some intelligence, and with her loving heart, her patience and her shrewdness, she soon established a happy relationship with her stepsons. She had three daughters, Isabella, Louisa and Jane. In the MacDonald family it was never 'stepmother' or 'half-sisters' but 'mother' and 'sisters' – a family united in love. Margaret MacDonald died in 1910 at the ripe old age of one hundred and one.

After a month's cramming at Aulton Grammar School, MacDonald sat for a scholarship, and won a bursary of fourteen pounds sterling per annum to King's College, Aberdeen University. The bursary system was meant to help poor scholars to higher education. Fourteen pounds seems a very small sum; in fact it covered a student's fees. He would still have to find his own lodgings and pay for his food and his textbooks. George could rely on financial help from his father; other students from poorer homes could earn money by teaching in their spare time. Aberdeen University went out of its way to help the poor student: fees were kept low, and the academic session ran from late autumn to early spring, leaving a long summer vacation during which students could hope to earn enough money to continue their studies.

The usual curriculum at King's College comprised four sessions, the first two concentrating on the standard academic subjects of Greek, Latin and

Mathematics. MacDonald had to miss the session of 1842-43 because of financial difficulties at home: The Farm was not making enough money that year to maintain the two MacDonald families in Huntly and a student in Aberdeen. He completed his studies in the following two years, however, reading Chemistry and Natural Philosophy (Science). He took the third prize in Chemistry and the fourth prize in Natural Philosophy. It is very likely that during these years he also attended some anatomy classes. His book *Alec Forbes of Howglen* depicts the life of a medical student at Aberdeen University, and particular attention is paid to the anatomy classes. MacDonald took his Master's degree in 1845.

How did he spend the year 1842-43? He had to find some means of keeping himself, so as not to be a burden on his family's slender resources. In several of his books he uses a large and neglected library as a background for his characters; and it is certain that he spent a period at this formative time in his life cataloguing and arranging such a library in a stately home. It is most likely that he did this during the summer of 1842, possibly at Thurso Castle. For a lover of books such as MacDonald it was a splendid way of earning a living. The library contained many books with which he was as yet unacquainted. He sampled the sixteenth-century poets and the medieval romances, and found many German classics.

He had already begun to read German, and so was able to tackle these, finding in them '*A mine of wealth inexhaustible*' for his imaginative development.

This library showed him what treasure lay beyond the bounds of academic scholarship, which at that time largely ignored English literature. In fact MacDonald himself was to play an important part in raising the study of literature to academic respectability, and was to be among the first Professors of English Literature in London. In later years his wish to share what he had discovered as a student led him to produce *England's Antiphon,* a collection of religious lyrics from the middle ages up to his day.

He returned to Aberdeen for the winter, and spent most of 1843, from February to November, teaching arithmetic at Aberdeen Central Academy, '*With great spirit and skill,*' as the headmaster commented. He never saw a vocation in formal teaching, however; possibly he disliked the régime in the schools of his day. His methods of teaching were far more advanced than the usual practices of the time. He was later to advocate teaching by discovery – something he would have found impossible in a school where other teachers pursued more traditional methods. In Aberdeen his interest in education coincided with a growing care for the underprivileged; he began to teach in the Sunday School of Blackfriars Congregational Church, and helped the minister, Dr John Kennedy, in his attempts to provide education for the countless beggar-children who roamed the streets of the city. His loving, imaginative spirit went out to these helpless waifs, and he carried into later life the memory of their condition. Many of his novels show concern for the poor and their plight. *Sir Gibbie* is drawn directly from his Aberdeen days; it is the story of a dumb boy and his adventures as an orphan in and around the Granite City.

The university period was critical for the formation of MacDonald's own faith. He was becoming more and more ill at ease with the Calvinistic doctrine of election, which made it seem as if God had deliberately created some people simply to doom them to eternal torment. His new acquaintance with the medieval poets and with the seventeenth century poets George Herbert and Henry Vaughan, made him think very hard about his relationship with God. They showed him a God who was all Goodness and all Love − a God he wanted to serve, if only it was true. In his perplexity he would often leave the town and wander on the Links or on the seashore, thinking deeply and praying for some enlightenment. At times his friends wondered whether he was going mad.

At this time there was raging in the Scottish Congregational Church a controversy over the doctrine of universal redemption. Students were expelled from the Congregational Academy in Glasgow for holding the belief that Christ's atoning work is available to all men, not just to the 'elect'. Mac-Donald took a great interest in the issue, much to the concern of Dr Kennedy of Blackfriars Church. The idea of hell as unlimited punishment was abhorrent to him, as was the notion that any soul in heaven could be happy while loved ones were suffering in hell – and if a mere man could feel like this, how could the God who is Love possibly rest while there is one soul left in hell? Calvinistic attitudes seemed to MacDonald to elevate the idea of sovereignty over the idea of love. The Bible, he argued, teaches that God is Love; people are mistaken in thinking that love and justice are opposing sides of God's nature. God would not be just to us if he did not love us. Punishment without love is unjust.

In moving towards a universalist hope, MacDonald did not give up a belief in hell. In fact his novels and sermons are full of references to it. Hell in his thinking is never a condition of physical torment, but of spiritual and mental suffering. It may be experienced in this world as well as after death. Indeed, what we call 'life' is really 'life-in-death', a living hell until the sacrificing love of Christ comes to awaken us, to bring us out to a new birth and a new life. Those who reject Christ in this life may need a further period of hell – an intensification of the treatment – to bring them to their senses.

He followed the Puritan writers and the Apostle Paul in declaring that the worst punishment that could come from God is for a soul to be left to its own sinfulness. *'What if hell be just a place where God gives everybody everything she wants, and lets everybody do whatever she likes, without once coming nigh to interfere! What a hell that would be!'* says Mary Marston in the novel *Mary Marston*. MacDonald insisted in his books that there should be punishment, but he could not see the point in its going on for ever, and he was confident that this is not the teaching of the New Testament. There are only four references in the New Testament to 'everlasting' punishment or destruction. The Greek word is *aionios*, literally 'of the ages', and MacDonald agreed with the theologian F.D. Maurice that the New Testament usage of this word refers to quality rather than to length of time. As 'everlasting life' – 'the life of the ages' – refers to the glory and the bliss of life with God, so 'the punishment of the ages' refers to the intensity of the suffering that may be needed to rouse some poor souls, enfeebled by wickedness:

'The sorrow, the remorse of repentance, they do not so much regard: it is the action it involves; it is the having to turn, be different and do differently, that

*they shrink from; and they have been taught to
believe that this will not be required of them there .
. . But tell them that . . . the torturing spirit of
God in them will keep their consciences awake, not
to remind them of what they ought to have done,
but to tell them what they* must *do now, and hell
will no longer fascinate them. Tell them that there
is* no *refuge from the compelling Love of God, save
that Love itself — that he is in hell too, that if
they make their bed in hell they shall not escape
him, and then, perhaps, they will have some
presentiment of the worm that dieth not and the
fire that is not quenched.'*

For the student in Aberdeen the merest possibility
that God was not the monster he seemed was enough
for him. In the glimmer of hope that came to him he
saw the person of Christ, and clung on to him. Hope
formed a large part of MacDonald's religious make-
up. It freed him from anxieties and led him to the
Source of Life:

*'Hope had ever been enough for me,
    To kennel driving grim Tomorrow's hound;
From chains of school and mode she set me free,
    And urged my life to living.'*

He found his life and freedom in the person of Christ

himself, and with relief gave up the notion that faith involved adherence to a set of doctrines.

> *'This is my quarrel with all those words and words and arguments and similes as they call them, and doctrines and all that – they just hold a poor body at arm's length from God himself. And they raise a mist and a fog all about him, so that the poor creature cannot see the Father himself, standing with his arms stretched out as wide as the heavens, to take the worn creature – and the more sinner the more welcome – home to his very heart.'*

The Father MacDonald thus laid hold of in the early 1840's at Aberdeen was to be his great love for the rest of his life. The expression of his faith matured and developed, but its contents never changed.

MacDonald had made a beginning as a poet while still at school, and when he was a student he poured his thoughts and feelings into verse. He corresponded with his cousin Helen MacKay from Banff, and sent her several poems. Her sympathy and understanding were invaluable to him in his spiritual struggles. One poem, *David*, intended as a companion piece to Browning's *Saul*, was published in the *Congregational Magazine*.

But now, equipped with his degree and his growing faith, he had to find a practical means of earning a living. He was interested in medicine, and had his parents been more wealthy he would have been a doctor. Science attracted him, and he thought of going to Germany to study with von Liebig, the famous chemist; but again he was prevented by lack of money. One obvious choice was the Congregational ministry, but MacDonald had severe doubts as to his suitability. Finally he decided to follow the example of many a poverty-stricken academic: he moved to London to seek a post as a tutor.

Dr John Morison, an old friend of George MacDonald senior, was then one of the most fashionable preachers in London, and he found a post for young George with one of the members of his church who lived in Fulham. MacDonald lived as a member of this household and taught its three boys for over two years before giving it up with relief. He found it hard to inspire in them any love for learning, partly on account of their own self-conceit. His position as a tutor, though better than that of a governess would have been, was unhappy. The mother seemed to resent him, and had to be conciliated at every turn. She took little care for his physical needs, although she might have been misled by his fine physique (he was six feet tall with the build of an athlete) into supposing that he was in perfect health and could therefore make do with the bare minimum. He was expected to take his charges to church twice every Sunday, which he found irksome. He was always, in later life, opposed to compulsory church-going. His letters home to his father revealed how hurtful his employer's attitudes were, yet at the same time he blamed his own pride and irritability of temper for his feelings. He was candid with his father, discussing with him the difficulties he found as he set out to follow his Master:

> *'My greatest difficulty always is "How do I know that my faith is of a lasting kind such as will produce fruits?"... My error seems to be always searching for faith in place of contemplating the truths of the gospel which produce faith. My spirit is often very confused...'*

While in London he visited his cousin Helen, now married to Alexander Powell, and she in turn introduced him to her husband's family at The Limes, an old Georgian house in Upper Clapton. Her father-in-law, James Powell, was a successful leather-merchant with eight children. The family was deeply religious and Nonconformist. Correctness in doctrinal matters was very important to them, as was devoutness in religious observance. The bright and bewitching Helen had already charmed the Powell circle, and now the introduction of her cousin George brought about a complete change of atmosphere. He first charmed Angela Powell, then in her late teens, by treating her as an intellectual equal, when her family considered her a fool for her inability to spell and her bad memory. He introduced the four younger girls, Louisa, Angela, Florentia and Caroline, to English Literature. Their reading hitherto had been strictly devotional, comprising 'hymns for Sundays and pretty bits for weekdays'. Now George MacDonald read them Scott's *Marmion* and Browning's *Saul,* then Wordsworth's and Tennyson's poems. He was a good reader: his Celtic sense of music as well as his own efforts at versifying helped him to put just the right stress and the right lilt into his voice. Through him the Powell girls came to see how restricted was their own denominational outlook, and how much larger their vision could be without hurt to their faith – indeed, to the great improvement of their faith. A passage in a letter to his father about this time might equally well have been addressed to the Powell girls:

'One of my greatest difficulties in consenting to think of religion was that I thought I should have to give up my beautiful thoughts and my love for the things God had made. But I find that the happiness springing from all things not in themselves sinful is much increased by religion. God is the God of the Beautiful . . . my love of

nature is more intense since I became a Christian
– if indeed I am one. God has not given me such
thoughts and forbidden me to enjoy them . . .'

Louisa Powell, who was two years older than Mac-
Donald, attracted him the most, and he soon began
to correspond with her, signing himself 'Your affec-
tionate cousin'. He confided to her his problems
with the family in Fulham, discussed poetry, and
before long was sending her some of his own poems.
Although Louisa always felt a great sense of
gratitude for all that George had to give her, the relationship was not one-sided. Louisa's sympathy and
encouragement meant a great deal to George; she
was, moreover, able to teach him such handicrafts as
sewing and embroidery. MacDonald was deft with
his hands and had the makings of an excellent crafts-
man. He found it immensely useful in Fulham to be
able to patch his own trousers.

The relationship deepened, but a tutor's life made
marriage unthinkable. After much anxious thought
and prayer, MacDonald decided to apply to Highbury College, London, for training as a Congregational minister. The first step, however, was to seek
his father's permission – MacDonald senior would,
after all, be paying his fees. He also wanted to tell his
father and mother about Louisa, and to discuss with
them his prospects for marriage. Accordingly, in

1848 he gave up his tutorship and returned to Huntly for the summer. He had a most enjoyable holiday: he played with his three little sisters, went riding and walking in all his favourite haunts, and shared a deepening fellowship with his father and mother. They encouraged his aspirations, and he was able, in the September, to enrol at Highbury College.

The educational standard of students entering Highbury was rather low – as a Master of Arts MacDonald was a notable exception. For many years Dissenters (Nonconformists) in England had been debarred from further education. University students, for example, were required to subscribe to the Thirty-nine Articles of the Church of England. By the beginning of the nineteenth century the Dissenting Churches had become aware of the lamentable ignorance of many of their ministers, not only in Greek, Hebrew and Church History, but also in how to prepare and deliver sermons. Denominational theological colleges began to spring up in an attempt to remedy the matter. MacDonald himself played a part in educating his fellow students. He offered to give lectures in Chemistry and Natural Philosophy, thus continuing his own interests and widening the other students' field of studies. As he had a degree he was required to study for only two years instead of the usual four.

Once he was settled at Highbury MacDonald

wrote to Mr and Mrs Powell, asking to be considered as Louisa's fiancé. They gave permission, although at this time George had no means of supporting a wife and had nothing to offer except his intelligence together with his eager, sympathetic personality. It is to Mr Powell's credit that he cared more about the faith and the sincerity of Louisa's admirer than about his bank balance. It was understood that the marriage could not take place until MacDonald had completed his course and obtained a post as a minister.

Congregational Churches were autonomous, each choosing its own minister itself. A church with a vacancy would invite applicants to preach, and if the sermon was satisfactory a trial period could be arranged for the intending minister, to see how he suited the congregation in exercising the full range of pastoral duties. Preaching was considered the most important thing, and the training at Highbury concentrated on this. The lecturers would arrange for the students to preach in neighbouring churches, to gain experience, and would relay to them the criticisms of their hearers. John Godwin, author of various commentaries on the New Testament, was MacDonald's Professor. He thought that MacDonald was too informal in his preaching and that he tended to be too poetical and intellectual in his exposition of Biblical passages. He also complained that MacDonald was 'doctrinally insecure'. This was an important point; the dissenting tradition, handed down from the seventeenth-century Puritans, laid great emphasis on soundness of doctrine. It is not surprising that MacDonald should seem careless in this respect. His own relationship with his Lord was an intensely personal one, and he had found rigid ideas of doctrine a great stumbling-block. How could the Supreme Person be bound by man's ideas of 'correct doctrine'?

Be that as it may, Godwin had to admit that Mac-Donald generally gave satisfaction when he preached. Satisfaction, perhaps – but it seems the various congregations wanted something more. When it came to preaching with a view to obtaining a permanent post, MacDonald suffered several disappointments. However, in the summer of 1850 he was invited as temporary pastor to Trinity Congregational Church, Arundel, and before long he began to think he would be offered the post permanently.

Louisa's mother died in June of that year, after a long illness. The family felt in need of a holiday, and Mr Powell rented a house for the summer in Brighton – most conveniently for visits to be made to the young pastor at Arundel.

On the third of October 1850 the church meeting decided to offer MacDonald the permanent pastorate, at a salary of one hundred and fifty pounds. Mac-Donald accepted at once, pleased with the prospect of being independent at last; and even more pleased to think that he could now make plans for his marriage to Louisa. He settled down to his work in the church, with a growing congregation both on Sundays and in the week. He held a regular prayer meeting as well as giving a weekly 'lecture' – this was in effect a sermon in less formal surroundings than on Sundays. He also began Bible classes, with separate meetings for young men and young women. He always got on well with young people, and was keen to fill a gap in the existing arrangements for instructing the congregation. He found himself fully occupied, for he was not one to neglect the pastoral care of his people: he was assiduous in visiting the poor and the sick. They soon came to see how deeply he cared for them and sympathised with them in their hardships and sufferings. They loved him for it.

The wedding was arranged for the following spring, and George and Louisa were eagerly looking forward to it. For Louisa's birthday, the fifth of November, many of her relations gave her 'housekeepingish' presents. But then came a blow which dashed all their hopes. George was taken severely ill with a haemorrhage of the lungs, and the plans had to be postponed. Louisa was in great distress when she heard the news, and was prepared to drop everything in order to dash to Arundel and nurse her beloved. But her family would not allow this: it would be most improper, they said. George was nursed by his landlady in Arundel. He had to lie flat on his back with leeches on his chest − a most uncomfortable cure!

After about three weeks MacDonald felt well enough to make the journey to London, where he consulted Dr C.J.B. Williams, an eminent specialist. Dr Williams diagnosed pulmonary tuberculosis and prescribed cod-liver oil, together with six weeks' complete rest. It was arranged that MacDonald should convalesce with his father's sister, Mrs Mary Spence, on the Isle of Wight. He went with mixed feelings. He did not feel ill, although he must have been aware that from now on he would have to be careful of himself. He was disappointed to be taken from his ministry before he had fairly got going, but he was learning to put his trust in the Father who loved and cared for him. *There is a reason, and I at least shall be better for it,* he wrote to his father. His pastoral work had left him little time for creative writing, and now he had an uninterrupted six weeks before him. For some time now he had been nursing an idea for a long poem, and here was his opportunity to write it down. By the new year he had completed a dramatic poem, *Within and Without,* the story of an Italian monk's search for spiritual freedom. Finding that mortification and penance lead him nowhere, he comes to London and marries. In the stresses of daily life, in the loves and jealousies of his relationship with his wife and baby daughter, he at last finds God. The poem is not a piece of Protestant propaganda although, given the feelings of the period, it might well have been. MacDonald is far more concerned with the individual. He agreed with the Calvinistic tenet that no-one comes to God unless the Holy Spirit first draws him; his own interest was in the means the Spirit might employ to bring an intelligent, sensitive, creative man into the Kingdom.

He now laid the poem aside to return to his pastoral work. Dr Williams pronounced him fit, although he had to continue taking the cod-liver oil. The wedding plans could now go ahead, and on 8th March 1851 George and Louisa were married in Hackney. After a honeymoon at Leamington they settled in a small house in Arundel, which Louisa's father had furnished for them as a wedding present. It was rented from one of MacDonald's deacons. MacDonald found preaching something of a strain on his lungs at first, and was obliged to spare himself in other areas. Louisa took a share in the pastoral visiting and, like her husband, endeared herself to many of the poor and sick.

In his preaching MacDonald was concerned above all with bringing out the practical implications of the Christian faith. He hated the atmosphere of controversy that prevailed in the mid-nineteenth century. Feelings against Roman Catholicism were running high in a reaction to the Tractarian Movement of Pusey and Newman; die-hard Calvinists opposed adamant Arminianists; Evangelicals fulminated against Liberals. It is not to be wondered at that MacDonald thought the daily outworking of the life of faith was being lost to view, and tried to remedy this in his sermons. In a letter to his father he wrote that,

> 'People have hitherto been a great deal too much taken up about doctrine and far too little about practice. The word doctrine, as used in the Bible, means teaching of duty, not theory. I preached a sermon about this. We are far too anxious to be definite and to have finished, well polished, sharp-edged systems – forgetting that the more perfect a theory about the infinite, the surer it is to be wrong, the more impossible it is to be right. I am neither Arminian nor Calvinist. To no system would I subscribe.'

In fact, although MacDonald disagreed with Calvin's doctrine of double predestination – that God has chosen, arbitrarily, some souls for heaven and others for hell – he was by no means opposed to the whole of Calvin's teaching. He believed firmly in the Providence of God – that God's loving care extends to every minute detail of life: there are no 'accidents'. He agreed, too, with Calvin's notion of Christian liberty: when the soul is set free from the chains of sin it finds its highest freedom in the necessity God's Spirit imposes on it of obeying the 'law of love'. He even accepted the tenet that was at the root of all Calvin's teaching, that of the Sovereignty of God's will; salvation begins and ends in the counsel of the Father and the Son. He could not, however, accept Calvin's argument (logical though it is) that if God is good, and he condemns some souls to eternal suffering, that condemnation must be good, albeit in some way that we cannot comprehend. MacDonald took issue with Calvin's second premise – how do we know that souls are condemned to eternal suffering? Calvin took it for granted from his reading of the Bible. MacDonald, turning to the same Bible, found much in support of punishment and suffering, but very little to convince him that *eternal* suffering is part of God's plan. Mac-Donald was no mean Bible student, and Calvin was one of the greatest Biblical scholars there has ever been. But might Calvin's interpretation have been limited by the assumptions of the cruel age in which he lived?

MacDonald's thinking along these lines was not yet fully developed, but by 1852 tension was beginning to show between himself and some members of his congregation. It was not simply a doctrinal issue. As in many dissenting churches the deacons had been chosen for their wealth and influence, not for their spirituality. When MacDonald preached against the worship of mammon, against cruelty and self-seeking, he offended a small but powerful group in the church. A rumour was current among the old maids of the church, who threw up their hands in horror at the idea, that their pastor had actually said that animals might share in the joys of heaven. To them this was going beyond the bounds of Scripture and therefore of orthodoxy. Had they never read the verse in Romans, chapter eight? –

> *'the creation itself will be set free from its bondage*
> *to decay and obtain the glorious liberty of the*
> *children of God.'*

Observation of the Sabbath was an important feature of the Puritan tradition. The eighteenth-century Puritan Jonathan Edwards as a student set himself the resolution *'Never to utter anything that is sportive, or matter of laughter, on a Lord's day.'* MacDonald's own attitude to the Sabbath was quite different. He hated to see it made a dreary round of abstinence and church attendance. His positive joyfulness gave great offence in some quarters. The following incident, taken from his novel *Alec Forbes of Howglen*, shows the joyless attitude that MacDonald met among the Congregationalists, as well as the sort of ironic reply he might have been tempted to make to them:

> *'Coming home with a great, grand purple foxglove in his hand, he met some of the missioners* (Congregationalists) *returning from their chapel, and amongst the rest Robert Bruce, who stopped and spoke.*
>
> *"I'm surprised to see ye carryin' that thing o' the Lord's day, Mr Cupples. Fowk'll think ill o' ye."*
>
> *"Weel, ye see, Mr Bruce, it angert me sae to see the ill-faured* (ill-favoured) *thing positeevely growin' there upo' the Lord's day, that I pu'd it up, 'maist by the reet. To think o' a weyd like that prankin' itsel' oot in its purple and its spots upo' the Sawbath day! It canna ken what it's about. I'm only feared I left eneuch o' 't to be up again afore lang."'*

To make matters worse, MacDonald translated and published privately some of the *Spiritual Songs* of Novalis. He had discovered the poetry of this German mystic while still a student, and had been greatly influenced by it. But to the Arundel deacons any expression of German religion was tainted with the new liberal approach to theology that was coming from Germany at that time. In their eyes MacDonald was dabbling in 'Germanism'.

Things finally came to a head when MacDonald speculated in a sermon that the heathen might be given a second chance after death. Thereupon the deacons visited him and proposed to reduce his salary. This was a blow to MacDonald, who was finding it hard enough to make ends meet (he now had a baby daughter, Lilia, to support as well as his wife). Thinking to himself that he would have to trust his Father to supply his needs, he agreed to the proposal. The deacons were nonplussed; they had hoped to provoke him into resigning! MacDonald's graciousness had brought their underhand ways into the light, and they were forced to discuss their grievances openly with their pastor. Nor was MacDonald content with this. The deacons were within their rights in reducing his salary, but his resignation was a matter for the whole church. MacDonald felt that it would be unfair to the majority if he should resign at the request of a few. A motion criticising MacDonald was passed at the next church meeting, but that meeting was attended by only twenty out of seventy or so members. MacDonald ignored it and carried on – with his reduced salary – for another year. Now it became apparent who were his friends. The poor, the sick, the uneducated, all rallied to his support with gifts of home-grown vegetables and even such delicacies as they could hardly afford for themselves. So the church was divided over its minister, and the breach could not be healed. By May 1853 MacDonald was convinced that the only way to unite the two factions was for him to resign.

2   A Wider Pulpit
(1853-1868)

It was typical of George MacDonald that in obeying
a spiritual necessity he should ignore practical considerations. His duty was to do the right and abide by
the consequences. His Father would take care of
him. MacDonald probably resigned rather sudden-
ly; however that may be, he found himself obliged to
seek a new position in some haste. In the South of
England he might not find a congregation ready to
employ a minister accused (by some) of unorthodoxy; MacDonald decided to try the North-west.

His elder brother Charles was in business in Manchester, and wrote glowingly of the opportunities in Nonconformist churches there. George and Louisa knew that Charles was inclined to be over-optimistic in his assessments, but there was another attraction in Manchester: A. J. Scott was Principal of Owens College (which was later to become Manchester University). MacDonald had already visited his brother, and found the life of mind in Manchester as a breath of fresh air compared with the dullness of the Arundel folk. Now he hoped that Scott might be able to recommend him to a post as a teacher or as a minister.

Louisa was nearing the end of her second pregnancy, and had to stay in Arundel. Reluctantly, MacDonald left her to the care of her sisters and travelled northward. It was imperative that he find employment quickly, for they were desperately short of money. It was only by Louisa's sisters paying rent when they came to stay that the MacDonalds were able to keep the Arundel house. George lived with his brother while searching for a post. He went first of all to Professor Scott, who heard his story with sympathy, and promised to help all he could. He was unable, however, to get MacDonald a post at the College. His help throughout the Manchester period consisted chiefly in entertaining the MacDonalds at his house, and in introducing George to his circle of intelligent and warm-hearted friends.

Mary Josephine was born in Arundel on the twenty-third of July. When Louisa was strong enough she began preparations for leaving. The furniture had to be put in store and all the debts paid before she could go to her father's home in London. From there she went with the two little girls to Liverpool. Her brother Alex and his wife (George's cousin Helen) were now living there, and they invited the MacDonalds to stay with them for Christmas. By that time George had had about eight preaching engagements, which had brought him in a little money; but no church seemed to want him for its permanent minister. He was not sure that he really wanted to serve in the Congregational Church. His experience at Arundel had made him wary of a system in which the minister is entirely dependent on his congregation. He was not in principle opposed to the Church of England, although he objected to the many 'men of the world' it admitted to the priesthood. What he really wanted was to form a church of his own, while deriving his income from another source. However, at this stage such an arrangement was out of the question.

In 1854 the financial situation began slowly to improve. MacDonald was trying his hand at journalism, and had a number of articles and short stories accepted by the *Christian Spectator*. Now he was able to rent a meeting room in the centre of Manchester and gather a few souls who were eager to hear him preach. He had hoped to interest working people, but for some reason he failed. The congregation consisted mainly of friends and acquaintances from his own rather intellectual circle.

The MacDonalds could also afford now to take a house in Lower Broughton. It was a delight to have a home of their own at last, and one moreover which brought with it a prospect of increasing their income. Not only could they take in a lodger (Arthur Francis, who had been a fellow-student at Highbury) but the drawing-room was large enough for MacDonald to use as a lecture-room. He began preparation for lectures in the summer, hoping to begin in the September. His subjects were English Literature and Physical Science; the lectures were well attended and great interest was shown, particularly by women. George and Louisa had a knack of making everyone who came to the house feel a member of the family. No doubt many of the young ladies took an interest in the birth of Caroline Grace in the middle of September.

The financial situation continued to improve in 1855. The *Christian Spectator* was still taking stories, and Longmans agreed to publish *Within and Without*. MacDonald found himself with plenty of work, writing, preaching and lecturing. *Within and*

Without was published in May, and the MacDonalds hoped for a holiday that summer. Louisa had never met George's parents, and they wished to take the children up to Huntly. However, there were difficulties. George's sister Bella was gravely ill with tuberculosis, and it was inadvisable to take the little ones. They considered leaving the girls behind in Manchester, but could find no-one suitable to take charge. When news came that Bella was dying, Louisa insisted that George go alone.

He had a bittersweet holiday in Huntly. He benefited enormously from the change of atmosphere. The clear blue hills of his home-land were like heaven after the smoke and grime of Manchester. The beauty of nature, together with the conversations he had with the Huntly people, provided a great stimulus to his imagination. But Bella, then aged fourteen, was greatly wasted away, and a sorrowful cloud hung over the whole family. MacDonald knew he would not see her again. He wrote to Louisa,

> 'That dear child Bella has been saving up her money for some time . . . and today she gave me two sets of flannels for the winter . . . Her little body will be cold before I wear them.'

Louisa, at home in Manchester, found life very

hard. She was expecting another baby, and had pre-natal depression. The three little girls suffered from all the usual childhood ailments, and were fractious at night. At a time when Louisa needed more sleep, she was getting less. The nursemaid, Charlotte, seems to have been of very little help. She upset Louisa by her rudeness, and broke the perambulator. Louisa had to buy another, which she could ill afford (she had been only just making ends meet). She was not without friends, but in her tiredness and irrita-bility she was unable to appreciate the good advice they tended to give out rather too freely. Her sister, Flora, now married to a Joshua Sing and living in Liverpool, invited Louisa to stay, but Louisa could not even work up much enthusiasm for this. How-ever, she did go and was no doubt able to enjoy something of a rest. She was cheered by the news that George had engaged an excellent nursemaid (recom-mended by his mother), who would return to Man-chester with him and take Charlotte's place. The favourable press reviews of *Within and Without* were another source of comfort. Charles Kingsley wrote an appreciative letter, as did F.D. Maurice, leader of the Christian Socialist Movement, whom Mac-Donald had met in London the previous year. In fact, *Within and Without* attracted much interest, although it made little profit for its author.

At the end of August MacDonald received the

offer of a post as minister to a small congregation at Bolton. This was immensely cheering, the more so as the congregation promised to respect his conscience in the matter of preaching. They were working people and so could not afford to pay him more than one hundred pounds per annum, but as they required only Sunday services from their minister, he would find plenty of time to pursue his writing and lecturing. It was probably MacDonald's immense sympathy with the poor and ill-educated that attracted the Bolton people to him; that and the fact that he never courted wealth. He often took the view that rich people are to be pitied because they lose out on the spiritual benefits to be derived from being poor. On one occasion in later years he preached to a congregation of rich Glaswegians; during the course of his sermon he remarked, *'One may readily conclude how poorly God thinks of riches when we see the sort of people he sends them to!'*

The work at Bolton progressed well, with a mutual respect and affection developing between the minister and his congregation. But in November 1855 MacDonald suffered an attack of bleeding from the lungs. He was gravely ill: the bleeding could not be stopped, although he lay on his back with ice-bags on his chest. In desperation his doctor tried the old-fashioned remedy of drawing blood from his arm. This seemed to work, and the blood-spitting stopped. By the end of December he was feeling cheerful and looking forward to a return to work. The doctor, however, ordered a complete rest for six months. Where would they find the money to keep them for so long?

George and Louisa had been learning through all their difficulties to keep their faith in the One who cares even for the birds of the air. Now they found their financial problem solved almost before they could begin to worry. Three men, only slight acquaintances of MacDonald's, gave him thirty pounds; five pounds came from a relative in Huntly; and the Bolton congregation paid him a quarter's salary in advance.

Things were a little difficult in the MacDonald home, with George ill and Louisa in the last stages of her pregnancy. As soon as the child was born (a boy, named Greville Matheson) at the end of January 1856, Mrs Scott took the invalid father to be nursed at her own home. When all the members of the family were well enough to travel, they went down to The Limes, the Powell's house in London, for a short stay. The period of George's convalescence was spent first in Devon and then, when the weather was warm enough, in Huntly. But as the autumn drew on George and Louisa realised that George's weak chest could prove fatal in a British winter. He needed a hot climate to restore him.

Lady Byron, widow of the poet, had taken a great interest in *Within and Without*, and had written to its author to express her appreciation. Now, learning from A.J. Scott of MacDonald's health and money problems, she offered to pay the MacDonalds' travelling expenses to Algiers. They would be able to spend the winter there, living much more cheaply than in England. George and Louisa thankfully accepted this offer, and made preparations at once. They decided to leave three of the children with Louisa's relations and take only Mary with them.

After a difficult journey through France — they had to spend a week at Valence, on the Rhone, when George developed brochitis — they arrived in Algiers in November and took rooms in a hotel until they could find a suitable house to rent. It was not long before they discovered on old Moorish house on a hillside to the west of the city. They moved into the ground floor. The first floor was occupied by the Archdeacon of New Zealand and his family. There were not many British in Algiers; the few who were there were drawn together solely on the basis of their Englishness. The MacDonalds found themselves in company with people whose outlook was quite new to them, and MacDonald was not sure at first whether he liked them. The Leigh-Smiths, three daughters with their father, were highly educated, intellectual, and advanced free-thinkers — a rare phenomenon in an age which prized women more as ornaments than as thinkers. At first MacDonald characterised them as *'Fast, devil-may-care sort of girls'*, but as he got to know them better he came to value strength of mind and character in women. The friendship continued beyond the Algiers holiday, and MacDonald was later to become a keen proponent of women's emancipation.

The warmth and colour of Algiers was a great stimulus to MacDonald's creative talent. He delighted in the variety of cultures that came together in the cosmopolitan city. The interest he took in the Arabs, Jews, Negroes and French was matched by the admiration they gave to his tartan plaid and Glengarry bonnet. He found much material for poetry, and before long had enough poems for a volume of verse. Longmans would publish it for him. He continued unwell, however, and had several severe attacks of bronchitis. No doubt he consoled himself with the thought that any one of these would have proved fatal in the cold of England. Louisa, too, was not entirely happy. She became depressed – a condition quite common in Algiers, and generally attributed to the Sirocco wind. As for the three year-old Mary, she contracted an eye inflammation that was endemic in North Africa.

By the spring they had to come to some sort of decision as to what to do next. This was a crucial moment in MacDonald's life. Hitherto he had let himself be guided by external factors, but now after six months of mental and physical relaxation he was in a position to determine his future for himself. Over the years since his student days in Aberdeen his faith in God's providence had been strengthened by the succession of events by which it seemed his Father was guiding him. Things so worked out that the way ahead was always clear, dictated by his illnesses or by his abilities. Now it seemed as if he had several options presented to him and it was up to him to choose the right one. The idea of continuing as a minister was receding from his mind. As early as Spring 1856 he had written to his father asking him to drop the 'Reverend' in his letters to him. He was still officially minister to the Bolton church, but apart from other considerations it looked as if his lung condition would prevent his living and working in the North of England. The interest shown in *Within and Without*, together with the ease with which he had produced his volume of poems, inclined him to consider the literary life as his calling. He knew he had many things to say to his fellow men, of comfort, of cheer, of warning; of God's goodness and God's love. If he was forced to leave his pulpit, he could reach a far larger public as a writer.

He could suppose that Lady Byron was still willing to help him financially, and he had no qualms about accepting what might seem like 'charity'. If he helped to *'Make life endurable or pleasant or profitable'* he felt that he had earned the money he was given. On the other hand he was not too happy about living totally as her pensioner (not that she'd offered him a pension as yet!). He was willing to work as hard as he could to support his wife and his family. He would try the literary life, supplementing his income by teaching and lecturing. If all else failed, he *'Would far rather take a situation in a shop than be idle.'*

George, Louisa and Mary returned to London at the end of April 1857. They stayed at The Limes for the summer; MacDonald wished to be at hand to see his volume of poems through the press, and it was a convenient place from which to look for a permanent home. At first they thought of settling in London, but George had another bad attack of bronchitis, which rather put them off the Metropolis, and they began to look for somewhere on the South coast. Meanwhile MacDonald made a brief trip to Manchester, to settle affairs there, to say goodbye to his Bolton congregation, and to the many friends they had made.

The book of *Poems* came out and was reviewed favourably. It was dedicated to MacDonald's father, to whom he felt he owed

'. . . the sense thy living self did breed
Of fatherhood still at the great world's core.'

At this time MacDonald also managed to make a
brief trip to Huntly. He was doubtful whether it was
wise; their bank-balance was still very slender, and
Louisa was unhappy at being without him. She was
expecting another baby, and was consequently in
low spirits. He was to be very glad he had made the
trip, however, for his father was to die a year later.
MacDonald had seen him for the last time.

Hastings was determined upon for a home, in spite
of Lady Byron's low opinion of its cultural and intellectual life. She gave MacDonald twenty-five
pounds and promised fifty pounds at Christmas.
The MacDonalds were able to lease 'Providence
House' for thirty-five pounds a year, and moved in
early in October. They felt that the name was too
pretentious for the size of the house, so they renamed
it 'Huntly Cottage'. However, it had thirteen
sizeable rooms – a large house by modern day standards! The drawing-room was particularly suitable
for giving lectures, for which MacDonald was soon
busy preparing. He also began work on another book
– a prose fantasy this time.

Christmas 1857 was particularly festive, with
generous gifts from the Powell relations, and the
fifty pounds from Lady Byron (she remembered her

promise, though very ill). Mary's eyes had not recovered from the Algiers ophthalmia, and she could only feel the gifts. She was very sweet and patient, and the other children enjoyed taking it in turns to lead her about. The MacDonalds would have scorned to keep their happiness to themselves. Besides 'little Annie', a waif who had become almost one of the family, they invited thirteen poor children to a Christmas party, with stories and presents from the Christmas tree. While they all had something to eat MacDonald *'Told them the true story of the day — about the good Christ-child.'* The happiness of the Christmastide was completed when, on the twenty-seventh of December, Mary recovered her sight.

MacDonald's love for children, evident in his early student days in his care for the waifs of Aberdeen, was becoming more and more apparent. He delighted in children. He was a master storyteller and entertainer, and could always rivet their attention. However, he and Louisa certainly had their hands full. There were now six children in the family, all under seven years. George and Louisa were untypical of many Victorian parents in that they believed children should be caressed and their emotional needs responded to. Nevertheless, they made sure they always won when it came to a clash of wills. MacDonald was not opposed to physical chastisement if it should seem to be necessary; but he was wise enough to realise that there should be no hard and fast rules. The temperament of both child and parent must be taken into account. The punishment of a child by a father of whose love he is sure can awaken him to the badness of his behaviour. In educating children, MacDonald claimed, we are working with God, not merely to prevent them from falling into sin, but with the ultimate end of making them incapable of sin.

1858 saw two deaths in the MacDonald's family. He had already lost, through tuberculosis, his mother, two brothers and a sister. Now his youngest brother John showed signs of pulmonary tuberculosis, and came to Hastings to be nursed for a while before going home to Huntly to die. No wonder that MacDonald called the disease, in grim jest, the 'family attendant'. Shortly after John's death old Mr MacDonald thought he saw his son's ghost. Himself not a credulous or superstitious man, this event perplexed and troubled him. Within two months he died of a heart attack. George MacDonald felt his losses keenly. He had loved his brother with the intense love of a Celt, and his father with all the respect and admiration due to one who had been a guide and friend from childhood. He did not, however, look on death as a final parting. In his later works he took issue with many Christians because although they claimed a belief in the Resurrection, they yet viewed death as the greatest evil than can happen, instead of the best good. His view was exactly that of Calvin:

> 'Strange to say, many who boast of being Christians, instead of thus longing for death, are so afraid of it that they tremble at the very mention of it . . . We cannot wonder, indeed, that our natural feeling should be somewhat shocked at the mention of our dissolution . . . This, however, let us hold as fixed, that no man has made much progress in the school of Christ who does not look forward with joy to the day of death and final resurrection.'
> (Institutes, *III. ix. 5*)

For his consolation MacDonald looked to his Saviour: as Jesus rose again and thus comforted his friends and disciples, so would he, MacDonald, be united in a joyful resurrection with his family and his Lord. He found moreover, that the departure of his brother and father seemed to bring them nearer to him in a new and spiritual way – just as Jesus' departure had brought his Spirit into the very hearts of his disciples.

The relationship between the world of the spirit and the material world was one in which MacDonald was always very interested. For him Creation was a Word of God; through it and by it God speaks to man, revealing mysteries about himself. Thus, while the natural world is not to be despised but enjoyed as a gift of God, its greatest value lies not in itself, but in what it reveals of eternal verities. MacDonald's next book, *Phantastes: A Faerie Romance for Young Men and Women,* was to explore this relationship and the means by which we may read aright the message of the material. It used the fairy tale as a medium to describe man's progress through life and the lessons he may learn. The reader is invited to puzzle over the hidden meaning of the encounters with monsters and battles with giants, and to make what he can of them. The influence of Faerie (that is to say, the Kingdom of Heaven) is all-pervasive:

> '*As through the hard rock go the branching silver veins, as into the solid land run the creeks and gulfs from the unresting sea; as the lights and influences of the upper world sink silently through the earth's atmosphere; so does Faerie invade the world of men, and sometimes startle the common eye with an association as of cause and effect, when between the two no connecting links can be traced.*'

The lectures given at Hastings were never a great success; but one good thing did come of them. London friends who heard him would invite him to give lectures in the City, and by 1859 he had a rising reputation as a lecturer in London's intellectual world. He began to make influential friends such as Russell Gurney – a top lawyer, the Recorder of London. He and his wife were friendly with many cultured people, and through the Gurneys MacDonald came to know such people as Matthew Arnold, Charles Kingsley and the Brownings. He had already met F.D. Maurice, and a close friendship was developing between the two. He renewed his contact with Barbara Leigh-Smith and through her made the acquaintance of Mrs Reid, founder of Bedford College. MacDonald's doctor came across an interesting case of stammering being treated by a friend of his, and so was able to introduce Charles Dodgson – Lewis Carroll – to the MacDonald household. Alexander Munro the sculptor was a frequent visitor to Huntly Cottage; through him MacDonald came to know some of the Pre-Raphaelite painters: the Rossetti's, Arthur Hughes, Madox Browne and later the Burne-Jones's.

The friendship with Lady Byron prospered and developed. George and Louisa made many visits to her London home. They respected and admired her for her calm of mind after her troubled marriage, and for her tactful help to those in hardship. She encouraged the MacDonalds to move to London, where MacDonald would find better prospects for work.

MacDonald felt that she was right. So many of his friends lived in or near London, and so much of his time was spent in the City, that the journey to and from Hastings was becoming inconvenient. His health had been no better at Hastings than in London; he would just have to put up with his perpetual attacks of asthma and bronchitis. They moved to London in October 1859, taking a house in Queen Square for six months while looking about for a more suitable (and less expensive) home.

MacDonald was offered now the Chair of English Language and Literature at Bedford College. The College, founded ten years earlier as a College run by women for women, was still in its infancy, lurching from one crisis to another. In many quarters it was frowned upon as lacking in propriety and orthodoxy. It was considered improper on the double score of being run by women, and of having male professors lecturing to the young ladies. The supposed unorthodoxy was largely because Francis Newman, the Cardinal's free-thinking brother, played an active part in its foundation. It was not always easy to attract Professors, nor to pay them an adequate salary. As MacDonald was a newcomer to the lecturing scene the post of Professor was attractive to him in spite of its low standing in the academic world. He was as grateful to Mrs Reid for appointing him as she was for his willingness to be appointed.

By the spring of 1860 the family had found a suitable house, Tudor Lodge, near Regent's Park. Although it was rather on the small side for the MacDonalds they were attracted to it by the large studio built on at the back, which would be ideal for a study and a lecture-room. MacDonald intended to supplement his Bedford College salary by giving independent lectures in his home. George's sister Louie came down from Huntly to attend Bedford College. She lived at Tudor Lodge, and proved a great help to Louisa, who was expecting another baby.

MacDonald had not given up writing after the success of Phantastes: far from it. But for several years he had to rely almost entirely on fees for lecturing and teaching, as he could not interest publishers in his writing. In the summer of 1859 he had begun work on a play, *If I had a Father*. Although he had a great love for drama, and had closely studied that of Shakespeare, in his own work he laboured moral and philosophical issues at the cost of dramatic effect. No publisher would accept the play.

The family was beginning to be short of money, and their situation became desperate when, shortly after the birth of Ronald, Louisa lost her purse on an omnibus. In it was all the money they had; the family was now penniless. Lady Byron had died earlier in the year, and they did not know where to turn. Louisa and George went into the front drawing-room to pray about their situation. They stood for a while, hand in hand. Then *'The postman walked up the steps, dropped a letter in the box, and with his double knock woke them from their quietude. The letter was from Lady Byron's executors enclosing a cheque for three hundred pounds, a legacy of which they had not been advised.'*

MacDonald continued writing. The idea for a novel was given him by Manby Smith, a journalist, who related seeing a strange epitaph somewhere in Scotland:

> *'Here lie I, Martin Elginbrodde;*
> *Hae mercy o' my soul, Lord God;*
> *As I wad do, were I Lord God,*
> *An' ye war Martin Elginbrodde!'*

It was a most striking epitaph — even blasphemous to Victorian ears. MacDonald mulled it over until he found the idea for a complete novel, *David Elginbrod*. It is a romance, ending with the happy marriage of the hero, Hugh Sutherland. But, as with *Phantastes*, MacDonald was using a conventional form as a vehicle for idealistic and spiritual ideas. The character of David Elginbrod he drew from his own father. Elginbrod is a spiritual giant whose influence pervades the book. He expresses Mac-Donald's own dislike for the 'Calvinistic' theology of the seventeenth-century Puritans, who give the impression that God's glory is just the thing that God himself is most anxious to uphold: that he would create men, feed and clothe them, give them wives and children, then damn them, all to uphold his own glory. Elginbrod concedes that the Puritans meant well, *'But, hech man! it's an awsome deevilich way o' sayin' a holy thing.'*

Perhaps it was these controversial sentiments that made all the London publishers refuse the work. It was only at the recommendation of Dinah Mulock (later Mrs Craik) that Hurst & Blackett eventually bought the copyright. They paid ninety pounds. *David Elginbrod* sold steadily, and MacDonald was at last established as an author.

For the next few years MacDonald was very busy writing and lecturing. The family moved in 1862 to a house in Kensington. Although it did not have a room like the studio at Tudor Lodge, it was in all other respects larger – more suitable for the still-expanding family. Four boys were born in this house – Robert, Maurice, Bernard and MacKay – bringing the total number of children to eleven. Their father could have wished for more. To people who inquired how many children he had he used to say *'the wrong side of a dozen.'*

In 1865 MacDonald applied for the post of Professor of Rhetoric and Belles Lettres at Edinburgh

University. *David Elginbrod* and a second novel, *Alec Forbes of Howglen*, had established his reputation as a leading portrayer of Scottish religion and manners. Many of his friends thought he had an excellent chance of being appointed. He supplied testimonials from such leading figures as Ruskin, Kingsley, F.D. Maurice and Erasmus Darwin (brother of Charles, the biologist). However, the selectors favoured another candidate. They wanted someone solidly orthodox, in the tradition of the Westminster Confession. MacDonald's own writings, together with his association with such liberal thinkers as Scott and Maurice, and such doubters as Ruskin, made it quite clear that he was not going to be bound by any 'rules' of faith. Louisa was glad about the failure. She was convinced that Edinburgh's frosts and fogs would be the final blow to her husband's health. MacDonald too was unperturbed. It was clear that his Lord wished him to stay in London for the time being.

He now took on the post of lecturer for the evening classes held at King's College, London, showing once again how his interest in education led him particularly to help the poor and underprivileged. The classes had been started with the aim of making further education available to a wider section of the populace. They were attended mainly by clerks and people in 'trade' – the very bottom end of the middle-class and the top end of the working-class.

'Further education' in this context should not be misunderstood. The knowledge most of the students already had was very limited. At Bedford College MacDonald had found most of the young ladies particularly deficient in Arithmetic. At King's, English Literature was a new field for many of the young men. One of the students, a bank clerk named William Carey Davies, became a particular friend of the MacDonalds, and for many years he devoted his spare time to dealing with MacDonald's accounts and secretarial work.

MacDonald's third novel was originally published as a serial, beginning in October 1865 in *The Sunday Magazine*. Where the first two had been particularly Scottish this, *Annals of a Quiet Neighbourhood,* was very English. It was supposed to be 'by the Vicar' – an account of a young clergyman's relationship with the people of his parish. MacDonald drew on his reminiscences of Arundel, omitting the controversial aspect of his time there. In the book he portrays the Non-conformist minister as a godly man who while disagreeing with 'the vicar' on matters of church government is willing to work side by side with him in caring for the poor and sick. In real life the ministers of the different denominations were more likely to be at loggerheads. MacDonald hoped to demonstrate that Christians of whatever denomination should lay aside their differences for the sake of the Gospel. He had himself left the Congregational Church and become a lay member of the Church of England. This was largely owing to F.D. Maurice's influence. Maurice was incumbent of St Peter's Church, Vere Street, and soon after the MacDonalds moved to London they began to attend his church. They grew to love and reverence 'F.D.M. the Good' as they called him, and they joined the Church of England mainly so that they could take communion with him.

MacDonald was nineteen years younger than Maurice, and respected him, as did many academics, for his grasp of theology. He joined with the working classes, too, in the respect they gave Maurice for his involvement in the Christian Socialist Movement of the late 1840's. Maurice had seen that the Church was failing the working man by giving him the idea that religion was divorced from 'real life' — that it was something for rich folk to do on Sundays. He and Charles Kingsley and Charles Ludlow had started the Movement in an attempt to get the Church involved with the working class. Workers' co-operatives had been established, but these had failed through lack of support. Maurice came to see that a lack of basic education lay at the bottom of many of the working man's difficulties and so moved into a field in which MacDonald himself was particularly interested. MacDonald had been present at the opening of the Working Men's College, which Maurice founded in 1854; he had been impressed by the speech Maurice gave, outlining his philosophy of education. Human problems could not be divorced from theological problems, Maurice believed; men needed to be shown how the truths of the Gospel could revolutionise their daily life. Biblical studies, therefore, had a prominent part in the curriculum of the Working Men's College. It is difficult to say whether MacDonald learned from Maurice his approach to education, faith and work as involving the whole man, or whether they came independently to the same conclusions. They certainly agreed wholeheartedly on this issue.

They agreed, too, in their rejection of the doctrine of eternal damnation, and in their concept of Hell as a place of terrible torment, albeit subservient to God's Sovereign Love. MacDonald included a portrait of Maurice in *David Elginbrod* as a clergyman who

'Believes entirely that God loves, yea, is *love*; and, therefore, that hell itself must be subservient to that love, and but an embodiment of it; that the grand work of Justice is to make way for a Love that will give to every man that which is right and ten times more even if it should be by means of awful suffering − a suffering which the Love of *the Father will not shun, either for himself or his children, but will eagerly meet for their sakes, that he may give them all that is in his heart.'*

MacDonald was not interested in politics, as was Maurice, nor did he share the latter's idealism. Maurice tended to assume that in an ideal state all men would be Christians, and that Church and State would function harmoniously together; MacDonald saw men as they are, and in his writings stressed the importance of each individual having a relationship with God. Both looked forward to a communist state – not a totalitarian state, but one where each man obeyed the law of love, and considered his neighbour's well-being before his own.

By the end of 1867 MacDonald had written seven full-length novels, as well as short stories, poems, a prose fantasy and a book of sermons – the first series of *Unspoken Sermons.* He resigned his post at Bedford College in this year, partly perhaps through pressure of his other work, but also because of a fundamental disagreement with his employers. Mrs Reid died in 1866, and her trustees wished to introduce external examinations, hoping thereby to raise standards. MacDonald was not alone in thinking that competition was harmful for young ladies (but he was more egalitarian than most: he thought that competition was harmful to men as well!). He resigned in protest at the appointment of the external examiner.

The house in Kensington was now too small for the full household of eleven children plus servants. In the autumn of 1867 the family moved to 'The Retreat', Upper Mall, Hammersmith, a large Georgian house with an enormous garden as well as outhouses and stabling. Now the MacDonalds could entertain their many friends in style. And the MacDonald style was something special. They did not go in for 'society' functions, but kept open house on Sunday evenings. A cheerful crowd of young people would gather to discuss current events, literature and the Faith. Greville MacDonald, then aged around twelve or thirteen, remembered the gatherings vividly. They were

> *'Often large, always happy. But no extra work was given to the servants, the family and guests together washing up the tea and supper things – "Your 'Day of Wash-up', Mrs MacDonald!" said Canon Ainger, solemnly punning, his shirtsleeves rolled up and a teacloth in hand.'*

The family put most of its effort into the annual day's entertainment they gave to up to a hundred poor folk from London's slums. Louisa would write the script for a play – possibly a fairy-tale, or perhaps an adaption of something like Dickens' *The Haunted Man.* The boys built a portable stage which could be pulled out onto the lawn, and painted the scenery (with the help of Arther Hughes' nephew, Edward). When the poor folk arrived they would have dinner, then go out to the garden to watch the play. The MacDonalds commandeered the talents of all their friends to help with the acting, the backstage work, the catering and so on. John Ruskin came to help, as did Lord and Lady Mount-Temple, F.D. Maurice's son Edmund, Canon Ainger, the Burne-Joneses, and many more. Tea followed the play, and the day ended with games and country dances. On the first occasion the MacDonalds were so busy entertaining the poor people that they forgot to provide food for their other guests – the helpers! But they organised things better after that.

At other times the MacDonalds went and entertained in the London slums. MacDonald would retell stories from the Gospels, couched in his own terms, which would rouse the interest of his hearers, the more so as it was only gradually that they realised the connection with religion. Later, with confidence established between MacDonald and the slum-dwellers, the whole MacDonald family would give entertainments, playing the violin or piano and singing. Nor were the living conditions of the poor neglected. Octavia Hill, a former pupil and friend of

John Ruskin, and a close friend of the MacDonalds, had acquired possession of a group of tenements, and was doing her best to improve the drainage system as well as to repair the fabric of the houses. In this she had the wholehearted support of the MacDonalds.

One or two of the more needy cases found their way into the household at The Retreat. The Mac-Donalds tended to collect waifs and strays, whether a broken-down old horse or an alcoholic and his fiancée. The time of their own poverty was past, but expenditure on such good causes was heavy. Mac-Donald had to keep on writing simply to maintain the bank-balance. Things were not so bad as before, however. As a writer of some repute MacDonald could now expect more money from his publishers for each new manuscript. His standing as a leading author was recognised in 1868 by his own university of Aberdeen, which awarded him an honorary Doctor's degree.

3 Mr Greatheart
(1869-1905)

Although MacDonald's reputation as an author was established, his time of tribulation was by no means over. His asthma, bronchitis and migraine had plagued him consistently, particularly in the winter months. He had a return of his lung trouble when, at the beginning of 1869, he went on a strenuous lecture-tour of Scotland. An attack of bleeding of the lungs, though slight, caused Louisa to dash up to Dundee to look after him for the rest of the trip.

That summer he was invited to join some Scottish

friends in a yachting cruise from Largs to Norway. He developed a tubercular condition of the knee, and spent most of the voyage lying in his bunk in great pain. When they arrived in Trondheim MacDonald was so weak that it was decided to return him to England by the regular steamer. They had to remove the skylight from his cabin and hoist him up on ropes to transfer him to the 'Norway'. The return to Newcastle-upon-Tyne took four days, and shortly after that he arrived at King's Cross Station looking nearly dead, to be met by Louisa. Neither Louisa nor George could believe that George's sufferings were pointless. Their loving Father had a purpose in everything, and it was up to them to look for it. Perhaps others would benefit from George's pain in the increased sensitivity it would bring to his writings, and the greater compassion he could show to fellow sufferers. The greatest benefit he felt himself to have derived from the experience was in being raised out of his cabin:

> *'The wonderful effect of the blue sky just above him as they laid him on the floor of his cabin when they took the skylight up . . . it was as if he looked out from his grave − the tall mast of the vessel rising from his cabin − that and the blue sky was all he saw − then he felt this Resurrection was come . . .'*

But MacDonald could afford little time to be ill. Even while he was convalescing he was writing. He was great friends with the idealistic young publisher Alexander Strahan, who had begun a quality magazine for children, *Good Words for the Young*. He asked MacDonald to contribute a serial story. *At the Back of the North Wind* ran for a year from November 1868. It is still one of the best loved of MacDonald's books for children. Its power lies in the fact that the fairy element in the story makes a real difference in the life of the little boy, Diamond. The spiritual world can be seen to have spiritual effects, and thus the reader feels its power to make a difference to his life also.

MacDonald took over the editorship of *Good Words for the Young* at the end of 1868 at a salary of six hundred pounds. But by the end of the following year it became apparent that the magazine was not as successful as its founder and its editor had hoped. Strahan thought it was because there were too many fairy-stories, although MacDonald disagreed. In his experience children never got tired of fairy-stories. He undertook to edit the magazine without salary. He wrote for it *Ranald Bannerman's Boyhood* – a 'real-life' story based on his own boyhood in Huntly. Perhaps he was willing to test Strahan's theory that fairy-stories were not wanted. But for his final year's editing he returned to a fairy-tale with *The Princess and the Goblin.* After that he gave up the editorship, saying that he would do no more editing whatever the salary offered. The difficulties of selecting suitable 'copy' had proved too much. He had lost at least one friend, who accused him of refusing his story simply to make room for one of his own.

MacDonald's books had now become extremely popular in the United States, although he was receiving no income from American publishers. European copyright laws did not apply in the States; the publishers simply copied MacDonald's stories from the books published in London, without reference to their author. MacDonald therefore approached *Scribner's Magazine* (New York) with the idea for his next novel, *Wilfrid Cumbermede*, and it was published simultaneously in England and America. Thereafter MacDonald published most of his books in this way, and made sure of the American revenues.

MacDonald's overriding commitment to instruct and edify his readers led him in many cases to spoil his work as an artistic creation by coming forward in his own right and speaking directly to his reader. He succeeded in his intentions, but the fact remains that his novels *as novels* are flawed. He once told his son Ronald that although he would have liked to write a pure novel, *'He was no less impelled than compelled to use unceasingly the new platform whence he had found that his voice could carry so far.'*

Wilfred Cumbermede is a happy exception to this rule. Because he wrote it as 'an autobiographical story' MacDonald was able to speak through the title character without spoiling the book. The novel's other main character, Charley Osborne, while not exactly a portrait of John Ruskin, gives voice to the many doubts and crises of conscience that Ruskin was confiding to MacDonald.

Ruskin was not the only doubter to find help and comfort in George MacDonald. Many people were disturbed by recent developments in science, particularly in geology and biology. The Church failed to give a lead in reconciling the things of the mind and the things of the soul. Scholars up to the mid-eighteenth century had been mostly clergymen who saw Reason as God's highest gift to man. But now for many people rational inquiry was leading not directly to God, but clean away from him. The Church began to suffer a sort of schizophrenia: Christians, thinking that Reason and Faith were at odds, felt obliged to side with one or the other. Many honest people gave up their belief in God because their reason forbade it. Others clung to their faith and stigmatised Reason as 'depraved'. It seemed to those who had lost their faith that these were denying their true selves and retreating into superstitious nonsense. On the other hand the 'faithful' looked on the doubters as wicked people who had given ear to the

Devil's lies. There seemed to be no middle ground.

Wilfred Cumbermede (together with the later novels *Thomas Wingfold, Curate* and *Paul Faber, Surgeon*) was written for just such a situation. It shows how a lack of love and understanding on either side of the argument could sunder families and lovers. MacDonald's sympathies are mainly with the doubters: they suffered far more than the believers, not only from the contumely of those who were more assured in their faith, but also from the agonies of conscience they went through. Some of them felt that death would be preferable to the life they felt condemned to, without a God. Suicides did occur. The Church, with its usual lack of sensitivity, propounded the traditional view that suicide is a sin. Charley Osbourne's suicide in *Wilfred Cumbermede* is seen by his father (a clergyman) as a final act of defiance against the Faith.

MacDonald had every sympathy with the despair of such people. He felt the logic of their position — indeed, he himself had felt the force of doubt, as he was to continue to feel it, on and off, for the rest of his life. He never had a full, confident assurance of the existence of God: he felt that this was more than could be expected in this life, for what room would there then be for faith? So he was able to draw upon his experience of his own struggles for faith, and the understanding he gave as a leading Christian writer was in itself a great comfort to the doubters. Moreover, his familiarity with the world of science gave him an added insight. He had no problem reconciling science with faith. He was familiar with the concept of evolution in the natural world and with the idea of evolution in the spiritual realm. 'Sanctification' can be seen as a gradual evolution – under the hand of God – from the soul's primeval filth and slime to its glorified state with the angels. As the physical environment is said to shape the different species, as God uses the soul's environment in Time and Space to 'knock it into shape', to eradicate sin and fit it for communion with himself. MacDonald was all the more ready to accept Darwin's hypothesis because of its congruence with what he knew of the spiritual realm. He did not, however, rule out a sudden conversion experience. Conversion, the starting point of the life of faith, was labelled 'Justification' by conservative theologians, who considered that Sanctification followed afterwards. MacDonald placed his emphasis on Sanctification. To him it included Justification: *'That man, and that man only, is justified, who puts himself into the Lord's hands to sanctify him,'* says David Elginbrod.

MacDonald saw that in many cases the doubters had problems because their faith was, to begin with, so weak as to be hardly worth the name. They were

Christians because their family went to church, because it was the 'thing to do', or because they lived in a Christian country. In such cases anything that made them question what they had vaguely believed and why, would do them good. Certainly, it could do them no harm. *'Doubt,'* he wrote, *'is the hammer that breaks the windows clouded with human fancies, and lets in the pure light.'* He held the old view of Reason: any form of rational inquiry should lead ultimately to God. Reason is God's viceroy in the soul; God's Holy Spirit uses truth and logic to illumine men and draw them to himself.

He also had some practical advice for those who were in doubt: even if you doubt the existence of God, even though you may doubt the Gospel record, try to do what you think would be the will of God if he did exist. Light will gradually dawn on your darkness. To a lady who wrote anxiously inquiring about faith, he replied,

> *'Though the Bible contains many an utterance of the will of God, we do not need to go there to find how to begin to do his will. In every heart there is a consciousness of some duty or other required of it: that is the will of God. He who would be saved must get up and do that will — if it be but to sweep a room or make an apology, or pay a debt . . . From your letter it seems that to be assured of my*

faith would be a help to you. I cannot say I never doubted, nor until I hold the very heart of good as my very own in him, can I wish not to doubt . . . But I do say that all my hope, all my joy, all my strength are in the Lord Christ and his Father . . . To him I belong heart and soul and body, and he may do with me as he will — nay, nay — I pray him to do with me as he wills: for that is my only well-being and freedom.'

In the early 1870's MacDonald received the greatest accolade of a Victorian writer: he was invited to go on a lecture tour of the United States. The idea was mooted in correspondence with Richard Watson Gilder, sub-editor of *Scribner's Magazine*, and the tour was eventually arranged with leading lecture agents, Redpath and Fall, for the winter of 1872-1873. MacDonald refused to submit press-cuttings or testi-monials as requested, thinking it was too much like self-praise. Redpath and Fall wanted them as evidence of his ability as a lecturer, to enable them to judge what fee should be paid. MacDonald was asking thirty pounds a lecture. He was perhaps surprised when Redpath and Fall agreed; he was not to know that this was low by American standards.

George and Louisa sailed with Greville, their oldest son, in September 1872; they took the Cunard steamship 'Malta', bound for Boston. In spite of very good weather Louisa was sea sick and kept to her bunk for the whole of the twelve-day crossing. They were met and entertained warmly in Boston, in preparation for what was to be a gruelling tour. It started quietly enough with a lecture in Cambridge-port on 'Robbie Burns'. MacDonald gave a second lecture on the same subject in Boston itself, to a packed house of over twenty-eight hundred. He was received with overwhelming applause; only Mr Redpath was displeased. He rushed up to the lecturer: *'See here, Mr MacDonald, why didn't you say you could do this sort of thing? We'd have got over three hundred dollars a lecture for you! Guess the Lyceums all over the U.S. 'll think they've done Redpath and Fall, sure! You make me sick! Yes, Sir!'*

The round of lectures throughout New England was enlivened by the warmth and hospitality of the Americans. The MacDonalds met Emerson, Longfellow and Whittier, and were lionised tremendously at all sorts of social functions. The weather was a trial to them, however. MacDonald's lungs were particularly susceptible to the sub-zero temperatures of the New England winter. Travelling was made difficult by the weather. Trains were frequently delayed by derailments and other hold-ups. MacDonald nearly died during a long wait in an unheated train. It was only through the prompt action of the guard, who brought him into his own heated compartment, that his life was saved. The tour was extended to make up for cancellations, and the Mac-Donalds were not able to leave the United States until May 1873. All in all they felt the tour had been worth while. MacDonald had not earned more than a thousand pounds, but he had won great acclaim from the American public, and made many dear friends.

MacDonald had not, of course, done any creative writing in the course of the nine-month tour. On his return to Hammersmith he settled down to work with renewed vigour. In the next few years he produced four novels, two long fairy-stories and a book of translations of Italian and German poetry. The 'family attendant' struck again, however. This time tuberculosis attacked Mary, the second child. George and Louisa were anxious to take her away from London, and took the old farmhouse of Great Tangley Manor, near Guildford. Louisa, Mary and the younger boys were installed there for the summer of 1875, while George continued at The Retreat, writing. The following two winters were spent at Boscombe, near Bournemouth, but by 1877 George and Louisa were so anxious about Mary's health that they decided she should be taken to Italy. They had very little money for such a scheme, but were so confident that it was the right thing to do that they went ahead with arrangements, trusting in their Father to provide for them. In the event they found they had enough money to take Louisa, Lily, Mary, Irene and Ronald out to Genoa. They settled in Nervi for the winter.

MacDonald was at first prevented from joining them. His health, too, was failing. He had been plagued with asthma and bronchitis for some time, and now at the age of fifty-three he fell ill with pleurisy. His situation was particularly uncomfortable, as the furniture at The Retreat was being packed up all around him. The family had decided to leave the place for good (it was afterwards taken by William Morris and renamed Kelmscott House). But MacDonald had to stay in Hammersmith in any case – he had not the money to take him to Nervi. He had been relying on selling his novel, *Paul Faber, Surgeon,* but his publisher, Strahan, refused it. He, too, was having financial difficulties.

MacDonald's dear friends Lord and Lady Mount-Temple came to his rescue. They brought him to their comfortable London home, where he could recover in some tranquillity, and pressed on him a gift of two hundred pounds. Strahan also rallied to the occasion. He found he was able to offer Mac-Donald four hundred pounds for the copyright of *Paul Faber, Surgeon* – less than half of what Mac-Donald had been getting for his other books. Mac-

accepted. Now he had enough to pay outstanding debts, to travel to Nervi, and to keep the family for the coming winter. He was cheered even further on hearing that he had been granted a Civil List Pension of a hundred pounds per annum.

The kindness of friends in England, and the joy of the reunion with the family at Nervi were overshadowed by Mary's failing health. She died in April, 1878. Her parents' faith and their hope in a future life did not lessen their grief at the loss of their loved one. To have experienced bereavement before was of no help: each new loss was as painful as if it was the first. Louisa, in particular, was inconsolable for many months. She had kept her anxiety at bay by concentrating on nursing her sick daughter; now Mary was gone she had nothing to cling to. Not even her husband's needs − he fell ill once more − could give her a sense of purpose. At last George wrote her a poem in which he lovingly reminded her that not only was Mary alive and happy, but that they themselves were getting near the end of life's journey, and could look forward to seeing their daughter again. Death was but the entrance to a greater happiness:

'We seek not death, but still we climb the stair
Where death is one wide landing to the rooms
                                        above.

The Italian climate proved beneficial to Mac-Donald in his illness: this attack was much milder than it would have been in England. The family decided to base themselves permanently in Italy. They planned to build a house to their own design, perhaps on the Riviera. Meanwhile they took the Villa Barratta in Portofino.

Almost a year after Mary's death young Maurice, aged fifteen, caught pneumonia and died after eighteen days. His condition had been aggravated by tuberculosis. *'It is a sore affliction,'* wrote MacDonald to his friend Carey Davies, *'but though cast down we are not destroyed. Jesus rose again glorious, and to that I cleave fast.'* His sorrows resulted in *A Book of Strife, in the Form of the Diary of an Old Soul,* which was published privately in 1880. It was a statement of faith and doubt, a cry like the Psalmist's after his God. Like the Psalmist, MacDonald cast his deepest feelings in poetry. The book is a long poem of three hundred and sixty six Spenserian stanzas, one for every possible day of the year. MacDonald longs for a vision of God, which he knows will give him the assurance he craves. But after all, it is God's love that matters, not his own weak faith. He rests content, vision or no vision, knowing that God will answer in his own way, in his own time:

'Thy great deliverance is a greater thing

Than purest imagination can foregrasp;
A thing beyond all conscious hungering,
Beyond all hope that makes the poet sing.
It takes the clinging world, undoes its clasp,
Floats it afar upon a mighty sea,
And leaves us quiet with love and liberty and thee.'

Ever since the entertainments at The Retreat, the MacDonald family had been developing its acting talent. Lilia in particular was discovered to be a wonderful actress. Bernard, too, had great acting abilities. MacDonald's success as a lecturer made him aware that he had some acting talent, and on his return from America he learned the part of Macbeth. Lilia played Lady Macbeth, and the family gave a very convincing performance of Shakespeare's play. All this was, of course, by way of family fun and entertainment. It was Louisa who took the decision to give a public performance. They wanted to raise money in aid of a convalescent home in Hastings, and did so by giving a performance of Louisa's adaptation of *The Haunted Man*, which they called *The Tetterby's*. So great was the success of this venture that Louisa wanted to continue. Could they not raise enough money in this way to help with the family finances? She dramatised the Second Part of *The Pilgrim's Progress*, casting Lilia as Christiana and George as Mr Greatheart. The first peformance was given at Christchurch, Hampshire, on the eighth of March 1877 – George and Louisa's twenty-sixth wedding anniversary. It was an unqualified success. The local press wrote enthusiastically about Lilia's talent.

Many godly people, however, were opposed to the staging of religious plays. Perhaps they were ignorant of the medieval tradition of the miracle plays; if they were aware of them they may have associated them with Roman Catholicism and opposed them on that account. They were unaware that even Calvin himself, when asked to sanction religious drama, pronounced in favour of it. MacDonald's own view was that the objection to religious plays was superstitious and therefore heathenish. The Lord Chancellor, unfortunately, was one of the 'superstitious heathens'. He refused to licence *The Pilgrim's Progress*. Louisa, not to be put off, carried on without a licence. She circumvented the law by arranging for *The Pilgrim's Progress* to be performed in private houses; she and the girls made curtains for scenery, and embroidered appropriate designs on them.

The move to Italy did not put an end to the performances – far from it, they continued until 1887. Every summer the MacDonalds returned to England and went on tour, George with his lectures, the family with *The Pilgrims's Progress*. By 1879 they were finding they could not stop it even if they wanted to. Louisa wrote to Carey Davies,

> *'I wonder whether you will be surprised to hear that we are intending to act our Bunyan's* Pilgrim's Progress *wherever we can. We have already made four engagements, the results of which will pay – and more – our journey home. But then we must have some more in order to pay our journey back . . . The Pilgrims has* (become) *such a reality to us that it seems a* duty *to do it – from the multitude of* testimonies *we have had to the moral and good of the play.'*

Many who saw it came away feeling inspired and uplifted. MacDonald's friends saw that the part of Mr Greatheart admirably suited the man who had been a guide and a friend to so many who were finding life's pilgrimage an uphill struggle. They began to refer to him as 'Mr Greatheart'. MacDonald himself was performing three jobs of work on these summer tours: he somehow managed to fit in lecturing with his dramatic performances, and often as not he would be correcting the proofs of his latest book while waiting in the wings for his cue.

The autumnal return to Italy was always something of a relief after the summer's hard work. The MacDonalds got the house they had planned, through the generosity of their many friends. They bought a site at Bordighera, and built a house which they called 'Casa Corraggio'. The name was an Italianised version of 'Corage', the first word in Mac-Donald's motto, *'Corage! God mend al'* – which is also an anagram of his name. MacDonald had always liked plenty of space, and Casa Coraggio incorporated an enormous living room, the size of a small church, where they could entertain. There was a large British community along the Riviera; many people would come either to the 'At-homes' on Wednesday afternoons, at which MacDonald would read and comment on his favourite literature, or to the informal services held on Sunday evenings. About one hundred people could crowd into the big room. The atmosphere was quite special, with the white-headed old man in his crimson velvet cap leading the worship. Louisa played a two-pipe manual organ which had been installed in the room. At the end of the service MacDonald would,

'Perhaps quite unexpectedly, rise and kneel, so that all . . . must feel their hearts opening out to God . . . And then came a blessing, wonderful in its quiet, deeply penetrating, almost tremulous words . . . then a deep silence, and perhaps the organ softly rolling forth Handel's Largo . . . Still and quiet even now, the guests would at last rise and go down

the wide stone stair and out beneath the flashing
stars of the huge Italian sky.'

The big room was also used for special effects at
Christmas. Louisa had the idea of representing
Tableaux Vivants – representations of famous
Nativity pictures using members of the family ap-
propriately dressed. They had no problem finding a
real baby for the Holy Child – as usual, they col-
lected all sorts of waifs and strays, among whom were
a mother and baby. The local Italians had never seen
anything like this before, and were most impressed
to see their own masterpieces so beautifully repre-
sented. The MacDonalds had an excellent relationship with the Italian population. They endeared
themselves to Padre Giacomo, the priest, when they
held a concert, the proceeds of which they gave him
to help build a church in the poor quarter of the
Marina.

In February 1887 a severe earthquake rocked Nor-
thern Italy – and tested the MacDonalds' hospitality to its utmost. *'The poor people have suffered most,'*
wrote Lilia ' – *their houses came tumbling about their
ears, some buried in the ruins.'* Casa Coraggio stood
firm, except for a stucco tower which MacDonald
had never really liked. As it was in a dangerous condition the household had to move down to the ground
floor. The chaos was added to by the number of

homeless people who came to them for shelter. The following day Louisa went into the church for a few moments' peace and quiet. As she sat at the organ there was another tremendous shock; she thought the whole building was going to fall upon her. Undaunted, she pulled out all the organ-stops and played the Hallelujah Chorus!

MacDonald was to include a graphic description of the earthquake in his book *A Rough Shaking*. Clare Skymer loses his parents in an earthquake; all they leave him is an unshakeable sense of right and wrong. Many of the people he meets in his adventures think he is at least a fool, if not mentally deranged, for not looking after himself better; but Clare would rather starve than steal. In vindicating Clare's standards MacDonald shows that the standards of this world are in fact 'deranged', and that Clare's are the only true standards. He had explored this theme in an earlier novel, *Sir Gibbie*, which is set in the slums of Aberdeen. Gibbie is an Innocent. Although he is a waif with a drunken father, surrounded by the dregs of Aberdeen society, his dumbness in some way seems to preserve his innocence. As he grows up he responds eagerly to the truth of the Gospel, and his innocence, backed by a new sense of Christ's righteousness, is a great challenge to the worldly-wise Aberdonians.

MacDonald had a great interest in psychology and

in mental illness. He anticipated Freud's exploration of the dream-world. Many of his novels include accounts of dreams told with significant symbolism. He was not alone in his interest in mental illness; some doctors were beginning to discover that it could be treated as if it were purely organic. MacDonald disagreed with this; to him everything had its spiritual dimension, and the human being particularly so. In mental illness he believed that *'The one central cure for evil, spiritual and material, namely the truth of the Son of Man,'* could effect cures as marvellous as those recorded in the New Testament. In a later work, *Heather and Snow,* he returned to this theme. Steenie Barclay, a congenital idiot, is kept *'Lord of himself through all the truth-aping delusions that usurped his consciousness'* by the loving care of his sister and parents, and above all by *'His unyielding faith in the bonny man.'* The 'bonny man' is Jesus Christ himself, whom Steenie sees walking with the angels over the Scottish moors. Steenie is less of an idiot than the world takes him for: his condition gives him an insight into the real world of the spirit. In his consideration of mental illness MacDonald suggests that perhaps it is the 'sane', after all, who are lacking something. Madmen may have a vision of things as they really are, not as they seem to commonplace eyes.

There were many sad partings in MacDonald's

latter years. Grace, the third child, died in 1884 of tuberculosis. Lord Mount-Temple, who had been such a good friend, died in 1888. Ronald MacDonald married that year and emigrated to the United States. He became headmaster of an episcopalian boy's school in North Carolina. After two years, however, his wife died. Lilia went out to keep house for him and to console him as much as she could. She returned in 1891 to nurse a dear friend who had come to Bordighera suffering from tuberculosis. By now the infectiousness of the disease was fully realised. With two brothers in medicine – Greville was a Harley Street physician and MacKay a medical student – Lilia cannot have failed to understand the danger to herself. Nevertheless she nursed her friend devotedly through her last days. Soon afterwards Lilia herself showed signs of the disease. That summer MacDonald was scheduled to go on one more lecture-tour. He was sixty-seven, and surprisingly fit. The family rented Stock Rectory, Billericay, as their base for the summer while MacDonald toured England, Scotland and Wales. He made a last visit to Huntly, staying with his cousin James at The Farm.

Lilia's health failed rapidly, and Louisa took her to Italy before George had finished his tour: she was afraid her daughter would be too ill to travel if they waited any longer. MacDonald wrote from North Wales,

'(Lilia) *has never taken care of herself, and now we must take care of her. If it should please God to leave her, we shall all take care of her; if not, we shall find her soon at the farthest. . . . A great good is coming to us all – too big for this world to hold.'*

Having given forty-eight lectures in fifty-eight days, MacDonald left England at the beginning of November. He was retiring from his work as a lecturer, and never again took a fee for speaking in public. He reached Bordighera in time to share Lilia's last moments: she died on the twenty-second of November, in his arms. She was thirty-nine years old. From her childhood she had been as a mother to family, friends and relations, and they all missed her tremendously. Her father could not tear himself away from her grave; he returned twice after all the other mourners had left. Louisa never really recovered from her loss. She was becoming frail, and by the summer of 1892, which was spent at Arth in Switzerland, only went out in a bath-chair.

Life was only a little less busy now the lectures were finished. There were still the 'At-homes' and the Sunday evenings in the big room at Casa Coraggio. MacDonald had taken up book-binding as a hobby, and would spend hours with paste and paper, vellum and parchment. He particularly liked restoring old, damaged books. He read avidly, teaching himself Spanish first, and then Dutch, so that he could read the works of the sixteenth-century mystic Jacob Boehme in their original language. He continued to read in Italian and German as he had done for many years, and he continued to write books. In 1895 his second prose fantasy *Lilith* was published. He had been working on this for some time. The story had come to him in an unusually complete form, almost as if by direct inspiration. He rewrote it, changing details of the story, but keeping the basic symbols and images. As in *Phantastes* MacDonald gives the reader the story, leaving him to interpret it for himself. It was not well received; the public had become used to MacDonald's didactic style and disliked this return to symbolic imagery.

MacDonald's last full-length novel, *Salted with Fire*, was published in 1897, and his last story appeared in the Christmas number of *The Sketch*, 1898. Entitled *Far Above Rubies*, it is a tribute to Louisa. The title is taken from Proverbs chapter thirty-one: *'A virtuous woman who can find? For her price is far above rubies . . .'* In this story of a young writer struggling to establish himself, MacDonald was remembering his own early years, and the tremendous encouragement he received from his wife.

Although MacDonald's bronchitis and asthma had greatly improved in the climate of the Riviera, he was becoming more and more troubled by eczema. He was losing sleep because of the itching, and getting more and more tired. He grew taciturn, only occasionally giving a sudden flash of his old wit and humour. He had to have professional nurses to attend to him. Then in 1899 he suffered a stroke, which left him without power of speech. His intelligence was not impaired, and his eczema cleared.

The surviving children had a house built for their parents at Haslemere, West Sussex, and George was brought home from Italy. The house was named after him, 'St George's Wood'. He would be taken for daily drives in the grounds in the summer, looking beautiful *'In his red cloak and white serge suit, with grey felt hat.'* There was a grand family reunion at St George's Wood in 1901 for the golden wedding aniversary. It gave Louisa great joy to see all her children, grandchildren, nieces and nephews. But she was worn out and ill, and died the following year. Her body was buried at Bordighera, alongside those of her children. Winifred and Irene, who were looking after their father, dared not tell him at first of his great loss. When at length he knew of Louisa's death he wept bitterly.

Winifred, who had married her second cousin Edward Troup in 1897, now took her father to her own home in Ashstead, Surrey, where he was nursed devotedly until his death at the age of eighty, on the fifteenth of September 1905. His body was cremated and the ashes taken to Bordighera to be buried with the body of Louisa.

He had lived through the whole of Queen Victoria's long reign. He addressed himself to the problems of his time, and by his writings gave hope and comfort to many. He also awoke sleeping consciences, and encouraged those who had laid hold of the Gospel for themselves to share their good news, not in words only, but also in deeds: *'faith without actions is dead.'*

BIBLIOGRAPHY

Chadwick, O.   *The Victorian Church*
                  (A & C Black, 1966)

Kendall, R.T.   *Calvin and English Calvinism to 1649*
                  (Oxford University Press, 1979)

MacDonald,   *George MacDonald and his Wife*
Greville   (George Allen & Unwin, 1924)

Maurice, F.D.   *The Kingdom of Christ* (Ed. A Vidler,
                  SCM Press, 1958)

Wendel, F.   *Calvin* (Fontana, 1965)

MacDonald,   *David Elginbrod*
George   (Hurst & Blackett, 1863)

                  Alec Forbes of Howglen
                  (Hurst & Blackett, 1865)

                  Robert Falconer
                  (Hurst & Blackett, 1868)

                  Sir Gibbie
                  (Hurst & Blackett, 1879)

                  Within and Without
                  (Longman's, 1855)

                  Phantastes
                  (Smith, Elder & Co, 1858)

                  Unspoken Sermons Series I - III
                  (Strahan and Longmans, 1867 - 1889)

                  *A Book of Strife, in the Form of a Diary
                  of an Old Soul*
                  (Published privately, 1880)

                  Poetical Works (collected poems), 2 vols
                  (Chatto & Windus, 1893)

In this series, by the same author –

George MacDonald: The Seeking Heart
Charles Spurgeon: The Boy Preacher of the Fens
Alexander Whyte: The Peacemaker